Travel and Tourism

LISA TRUESDALE

LIGHTBOX
openlightbox.com

LIGHTBOX

Go to
www.openlightbox.com
and enter this book's
unique code.

ACCESS CODE

LBXR3653

Lightbox is an all-inclusive digital solution for the teaching and learning of curriculum topics in an original, groundbreaking way. Lightbox is based on National Curriculum Standards.

STANDARD FEATURES OF LIGHTBOX

AUDIO High-quality narration using text-to-speech system

ACTIVITIES Printable PDFs that can be emailed and graded

SLIDESHOWS Pictorial overviews of key concepts

VIDEOS Embedded high-definition video clips

WEBLINKS Curated links to external, child-safe resources

TRANSPARENCIES Step-by-step layering of maps, diagrams, charts, and timelines

INTERACTIVE MAPS Interactive maps and aerial satellite imagery

QUIZZES Ten multiple choice questions that are automatically graded and emailed for teacher assessment

KEY WORDS Matching key concepts to their definitions

CONTENTS

Travel and Tourism in the United States

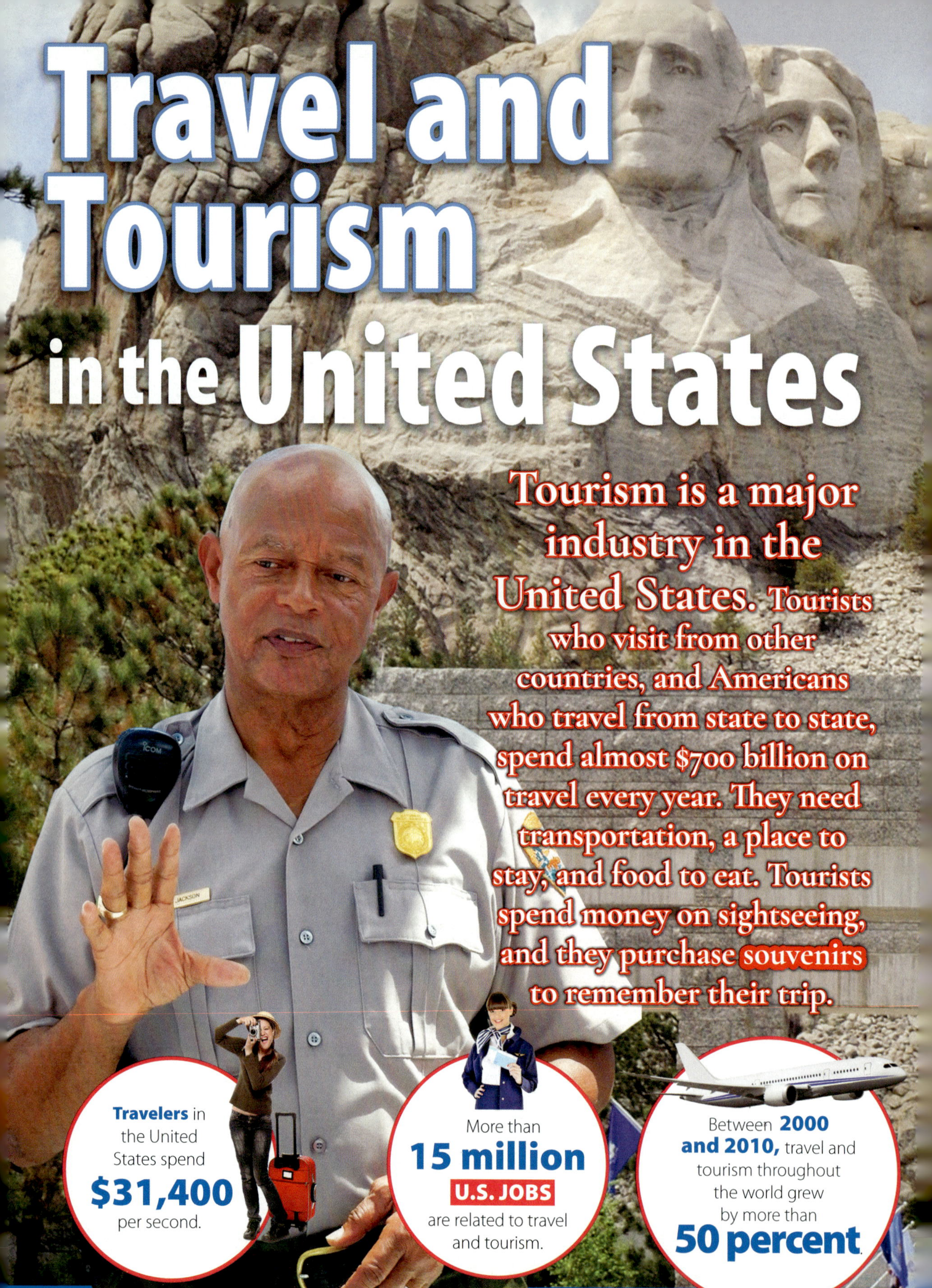

Tourism is a major industry in the United States. Tourists who visit from other countries, and Americans who travel from state to state, spend almost $700 billion on travel every year. They need transportation, a place to stay, and food to eat. Tourists spend money on sightseeing, and they purchase **souvenirs** to remember their trip.

Travelers in the United States spend **$31,400** per second.

More than **15 million** **U.S. JOBS** are related to travel and tourism.

Between **2000 and 2010,** travel and tourism throughout the world grew by more than **50 percent**.

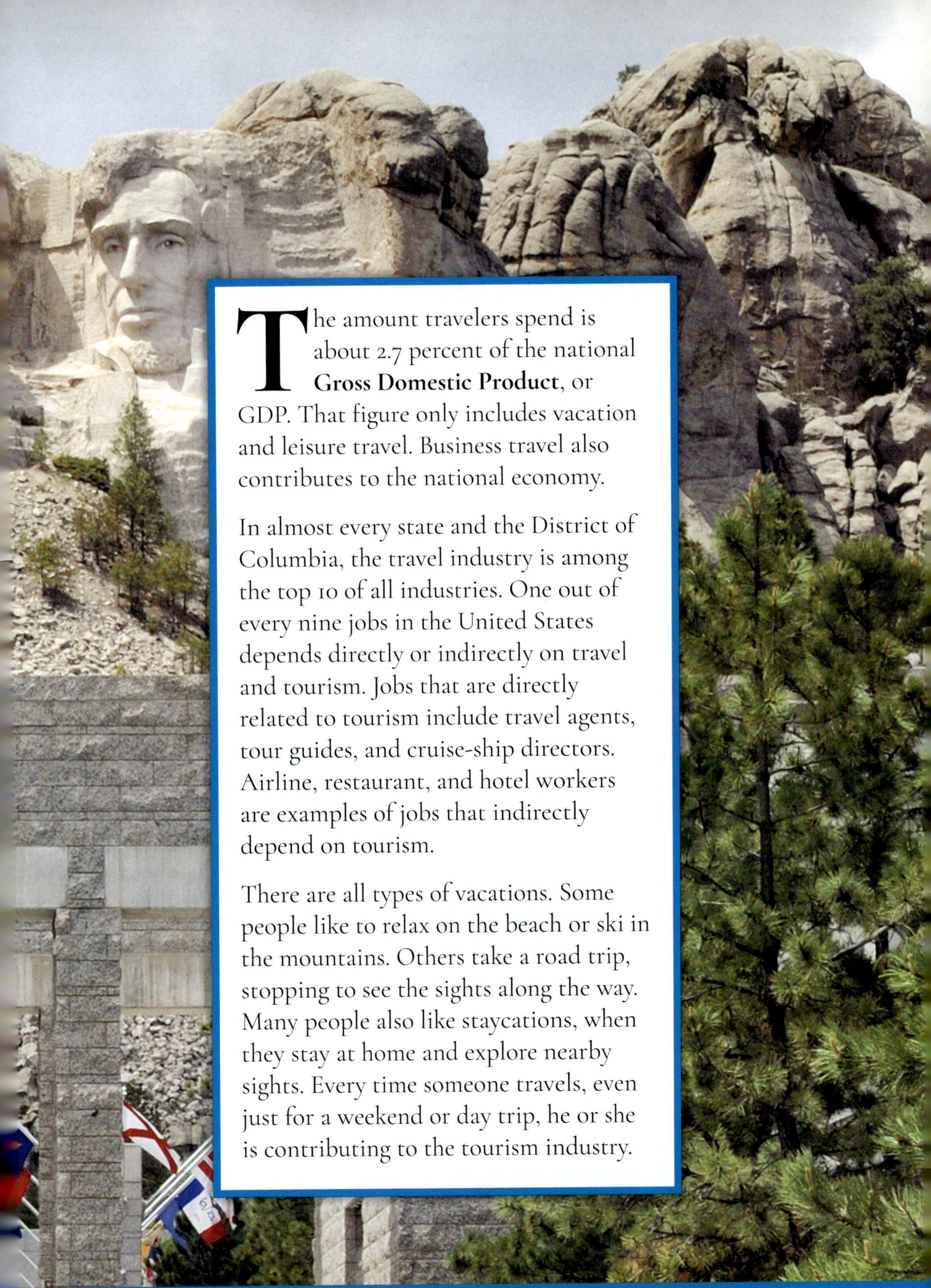

The amount travelers spend is about 2.7 percent of the national **Gross Domestic Product**, or GDP. That figure only includes vacation and leisure travel. Business travel also contributes to the national economy.

In almost every state and the District of Columbia, the travel industry is among the top 10 of all industries. One out of every nine jobs in the United States depends directly or indirectly on travel and tourism. Jobs that are directly related to tourism include travel agents, tour guides, and cruise-ship directors. Airline, restaurant, and hotel workers are examples of jobs that indirectly depend on tourism.

There are all types of vacations. Some people like to relax on the beach or ski in the mountains. Others take a road trip, stopping to see the sights along the way. Many people also like staycations, when they stay at home and explore nearby sights. Every time someone travels, even just for a weekend or day trip, he or she is contributing to the tourism industry.

Travel and Tourism Then and Now

Advancements in transportation have been the biggest boost to the travel and tourism industry over the past 200 years. Now, travelers do not have to spend so much of their vacation getting to where they are going. They can spend more time enjoying their destination.

Coast to Coast

In the 1700s, a trip from the east coast to the west coast took several months by horse and wagon. Today, an airplane can fly from New York City to San Francisco in about five or six hours.

THEN

NOW

Where to Stay

In the 1800s, most hotels were fancy, and only wealthy people could afford to stay in them. Today, travelers have many affordable choices, such as motels, campgrounds, and **hostels**.

THEN

NOW

In 1800, traveling from New York City to Illinois on a steam-powered train took about five weeks. In 1857, because of railroad improvements, the same train trip took just two days. In the 1940s, airplanes offered an even faster way to travel.

Travelers today also have more choices of where to stay once they arrive at their destination. In the 1930s and 1940s, hotels began offering **amenities** to entice travelers, such as air conditioning and TVs in the rooms, and swimming pools for guests to enjoy. There are now more than 52,000 hotels in the United States, with a total of more than 5 million individual rooms.

Booking Accommodation

In the past, people would write letters to hotels to request rooms or just walk in and request a room. Today, most people book their hotel online, using a booking company or the hotel's website.

THEN

NOW

Group Travel

When people went on trips in the past, they often traveled with friends and family. Today, people can book package tours with travel companies and vacation with people they have never met before.

THEN

NOW

Popular Places in the United States

The United States has a wide range of attractions for people to visit. Some allow people to experience nature, while others involve city stays. The country's most popular destinations are spread out across the country.

1 New York City
New York

New York attracts about 39 million visitors a year. The city offers attractions for all types of people. Some popular sites are free to visit, such as Central Park, Times Square, and Grand Central Station.

2 Hawaiian Islands
Hawaii

More than 9 million people visited the Hawaiian Islands in 2017. Most came to take in the tropical weather, sandy beaches, and Hawaiian culture. Popular attractions include Pearl Harbor and Volcanoes National Park.

to Visit

3 Las Vegas
Nevada

Almost 40 million people visit Las Vegas each year. Visitors can dine at top restaurants and watch concerts by the world's leading performers. Some play games of chance at the city's many **casinos**.

4 Orlando
Florida

Orlando draws in millions of visitors every year. The city is home to two of the country's best-known theme parks, Walt Disney World and Universal Studios. Other nearby attractions include SeaWorld and Gatorland.

Tourism Sectors Ranked by Importance

Tourism contributes about $683.1 billion to the U.S. economy each year. However, the tourism industry also contributes to GDP through its effect on other industries. The retail industry, for instance, benefits when tourists shop in its stores for souvenirs or clothing. When this indirect contribution is taken into account, tourism actually puts more than $1 trillion into the U.S. economy. That is about 8.1 percent of the GDP.

Air travel is an important way of getting around. There are about 5,000 airplanes in America's skies at any given time.

The tourism industry itself has three main sectors that account for more than 45 percent of the industry's earnings. The largest of these sectors is accommodation. It accounts for about 20 percent of all spending by foreign visitors in the United States. In 2016 alone, visitors spent more than $293 billion on hotels and other accommodation outlets.

In **2016**, an average of **42,700** flights landed at U.S. airports every day.

The number of jobs in the travel industry has grown by **16.6 percent** since **2010**.

The number of visitors to the **United States** from China is expected to grow by **121 percent** by **2021**.

Top 10 Sources of International Visitors to the United States, 2016

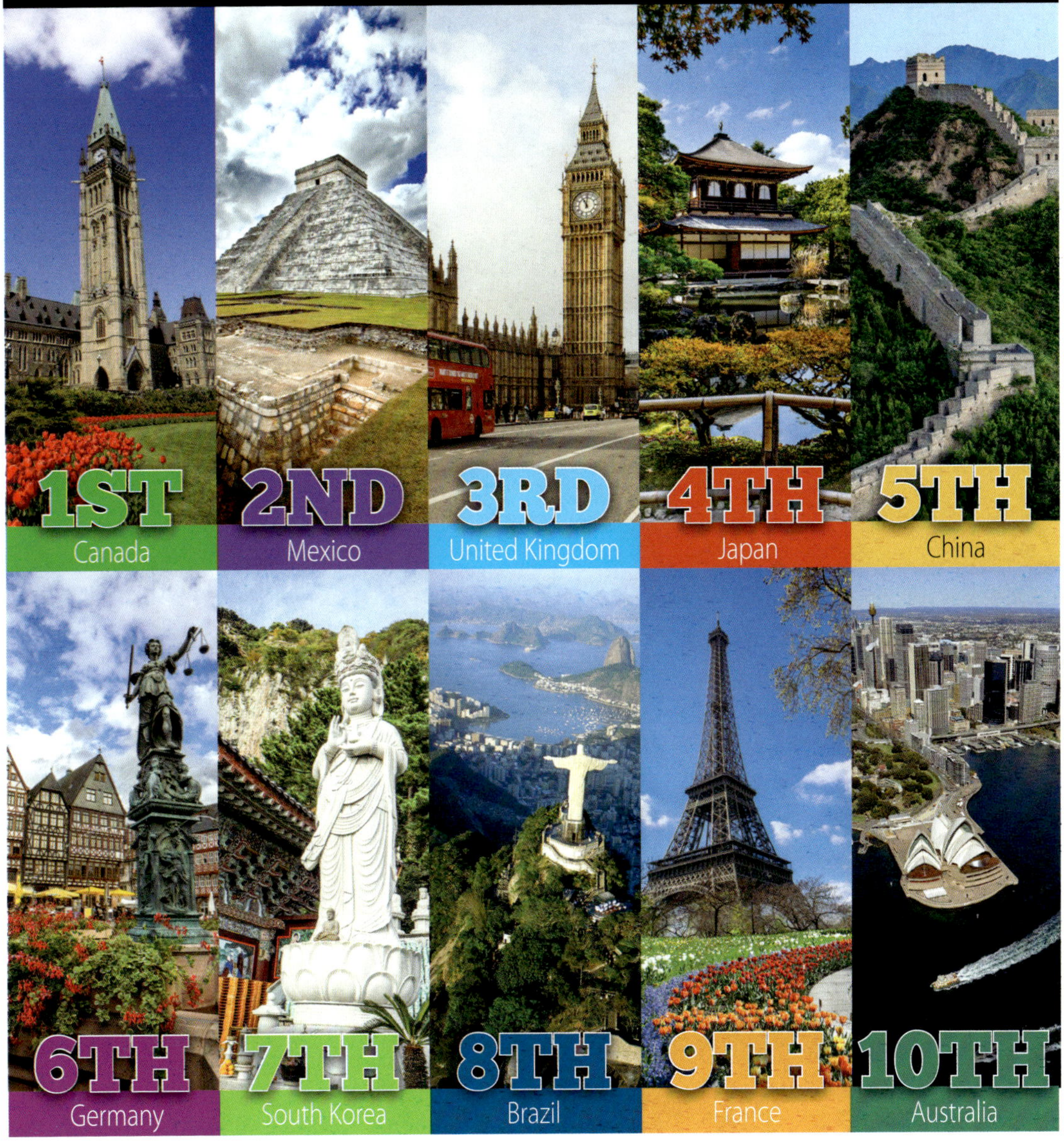

After accommodation, air travel is the second largest sector of the tourist industry. Food services make up the third largest sector. Travelers to destinations in the United States spent about $226 million on air travel in 2016. They spent another $174 billion on food and drinks once they arrived in the country. These figures accounted for about 15 percent and 11 percent, respectively, of total tourist spending in the United States for the year. California is the most visited state.

Timeline of Travel and Tourism

Travel has a long history. Tourism, or traveling for vacations, only began in the late 1800s. Travel and tourism have been changed by developments in transportation and communications.

1850	1870	1900	1905	1910

1869. The first transcontinental railroad line connects New York City and San Francisco. A train trip between the two cities takes less than a week.

1872. Yellowstone National Park, in Wyoming, Montana, and Idaho, is the first national park established in the United States. About 300 people visit during the first year.

1908. Wilbur Wright, one of the inventors of the first successful airplane, takes an employee for a ride. This is considered to be the world's first passenger flight.

1917. Chalks Ocean Airways becomes the first major U.S. airline. It operates between Florida and the Bahamas until 2017.

1955. Disneyland opens in southern California. It is still one of the most popular theme parks in the country today.

Future. Artificial intelligence machines will take over many functions in tourism, such as room service in hotels. Methods of transportation will grow faster still.

1920 | **1930** | **1960** | **1995** | **THE FUTURE**

1925. The first motel in the world opens in San Luis Obispo, California. The name "motel" comes from a combination of "motor" and "hotel." A motel was like a hotel, but it was created especially for car drivers.

1995. The first airline tickets are sold on the internet. This innovation marks the beginning of the decline of travel agencies.

International Travel and the United States

More than 75 million people visit the United States annually from other countries, and the number continues to grow every year. The average international visitor stays for 18 nights and spends more than $4,000. Shopping and sightseeing are the two most popular activities for tourists from other countries.

Many people buy luggage with hard cases and wheels to protect their belongings and make them easier to move.

In 2016, more than 80 million U.S. citizens traveled to other countries. Almost half went to either Mexico or Canada. The rest left the continent completely. Europe was the third most popular destination, followed by the Caribbean and Asia. Most of a U.S. traveler's budget spent in the country they are visiting goes toward food, lodging, and souvenirs. Expenses for these international trips also contribute to the U.S. economy. Airfare is often paid to a U.S.-based airline, and tourists purchase goods in the United States before they leave, such as suitcases and clothing. They also pay fees for passports and other official travel documents.

The **UNITED STATES** is the **SECOND MOST** visited country in the world. France is the **FIRST**.

Almost **40 percent** of U.S. residents have a valid **PASSPORT.**

The number **ONE** most popular international destination for U.S. travelers is **Mexico.**

Travelers from the United States visit Mexico to enjoy its atmosphere, its food, its old cities, and its lively markets.

Facing the Issues

On September 11, 2001, terrorists hijacked airliners and flew them into targets in New York City and Washington, D.C. Since then, security has become a major issue for the travel industry. All air passengers are screened before they are allowed to board. They are forbidden from carrying anything that might be used as a weapon, such as knives or liquids that could contain explosives. In addition, law enforcement personnel guard tourist sites where people gather, which might become targets for terrorist attacks.

Another problem facing the travel industry is **globalization**. Hotels, stores, and restaurants are becoming similar around the country and around the world. This makes it more difficult for resorts to offer visitors a unique experience that they will remember or recommend to their friends.

Armed police patrol airports to prevent terrorist attacks. Many police forces have aviation or airport departments with specialized antiterrorism training.

Debate

The threat of terrorism impacts all forms of travel. Air passengers now face long lines to pass through security. This adds time and inconvenience to their journey. Has airport security become so intrusive that it makes people more reluctant to travel by air?

YES

- Long delays at security add hours to journeys. This is a great inconvenience to passengers
- Many passengers object that body scanners and being patted down are intrusions into their privacy.

NO

- Everyone accepts that delays are worthwhile to make sure dangerous passengers cannot board a flight.
- People's right to security onboard an airplane is more important than people's right to privacy.

In 2017, there were 38,745 rooms available in private homes for visitors arriving in New York City.

Looking to the Future

The travel and tourism industry of today does not look anything like it did 100 years ago or even 50 years ago. Transportation is much faster today, and it will continue to get faster in the future. Aerospace companies are working on **supersonic** jets that will cut the travel time from New York to London in half. U.S. engineers are working on Hyperloop One, a transportation system that will allow people to travel through tubes in containers called pods. Hyperloop One is expected to travel 700 miles per hour (1,126 kilometers per hour), which is about 125 miles per hour (201 kph) quicker than the fastest airplanes. A Hyperloop passenger will be able to travel from Los Angeles to Las Vegas in 30 minutes. It currently takes more than five hours by car.

Accommodation is also changing. Hotels face competition from the **sharing economy**. Websites allow visitors to find accommodation in private homes. Visitors can choose to rent a whole lodging or to share with the owner. The rooms are usually cheaper than accommodation in hotels. Property owners still make more money from short-term rentals like this than from renting to permanent tenants.

In addition, websites allow users to create their own holidays. That means travelers no longer need travel agents. They can use a single site to find accommodation, arrange transportation, and even book excursions or activities.

Hyperloop One aims to move people and goods inside pods through long tubes. The first Hyperloop One is scheduled to connect Los Angeles and Las Vegas by 2021.

Careers in Travel and Tourism

Some travel careers are directly related to the industry, such as a travel agent who helps people plan a vacation. A career can also be indirectly related to the travel industry. Such careers include cooks who work at restaurants that serve both tourists and local residents.

Travel Agent
Even with the internet, people still use travel agents to help plan vacations. Travel agents work with airlines and hotels, so they often know about discounts that cannot be found online. Business travelers often use travel agencies because they do not have time to plan their own trips.

Duties: Planning vacations, booking transportation and hotel reservations

Education: A degree or college course in communications and business. Some agencies give specialized training.

Interests: Working with people, traveling, finding creative solutions, budgeting

Tourism Promoter
Tourism promoters work for a specific town, city, state, or region to help bring people to the area. They may work in a tourism office or at a counter in the local bus or railroad station or airport. Like a travel agent, they sometimes help potential visitors plan a customized trip.

Duties: Handing out brochures, giving advice, preparing marketing materials

Education: A degree or college course in communications, marketing, journalism, or public relations

Interests: Working with people, traveling, writing, promoting a local area

Tour Guide
Tour companies offer guided trips that include lodging, transportation, food, and sightseeing. These tours can be general or can cater to interests such as skiing. A tour guide is responsible for the group throughout the tour, helping to make people feel safe and comfortable.

Duties: Guiding travelers through a daily **itinerary** and keeping a tour on schedule

Education: For specialized tours, guides need in-depth knowledge of the activity.

Interests: Leadership, business, and managing people

Activity

Plan your own dream vacation

Is there a place you have always wanted to travel to? What about the rest of your family? Your project is to be the travel agent for your family's next vacation. As you plan every detail, you will become an expert about the destination. Perhaps your family will like the idea so much that you will actually get to go someday.

You will need:

- Notebook or paper
- Pen or pencil to take notes
- Construction paper
- Colored pencils
- Access to the internet
- Photos or illustrations printed from the internet

Instructions

1. Interview your family members about locations they might like to visit. It could be somewhere inside the United States or a destination in a foreign country. Take into account everyone's preferences before choosing a single destination.
2. Once you choose a single destination, research it thoroughly. Look through travel guidebooks at the public library, and search on the internet. Make a list of all the sights and attractions you would like to see when you are there.
5. When your research is completed, use your list to prepare your own brochure for the destination using the construction paper, colored pencils, and printed photos. Add interesting information about what there is to see and do.
6. Present the brochure to your family and tell them all about the trip you planned.

Quiz

Check out how much you have learned about travel and tourism in the United States. The answers to all these questions are in this book.

ONE
How many flights land at U.S. airports every day?

TWO
Which two parts of a vacation usually cost the most?

THREE
Which U.S. state is visited the most?

FOUR
What is a staycation?

FIVE
How many people visited the Hawaiian Islands in 2017?

SIX
What is the name of a person whose job is to plans trips for people?

SEVEN
How fast will Hyperloop One be able to travel?

EIGHT
How long did a train ride take from New York to Illinois in the year 1800?

NINE
Why do business travelers often use travel agents?

TEN
Which two countries see the most tourists from the United States?

ANSWERS

ONE 42,700 **TWO** Air travel and lodging. **THREE** California **FOUR** When someone acts like a tourist at home **FIVE** More than 9 million **SIX** A travel agent **SEVEN** 700 miles per hour (1,126 km/h) **EIGHT** About five weeks. **NINE** They do not have time to plan their own trips. **TEN** Mexico and Canada

Key Words

amenities: special touches that make a place or occasion more convenient or enjoyable

casinos: buildings where games of chance are played

globalization: growth to a global or worldwide scale

gross domestic product (GDP): the dollar value of all goods and services produced in a given time and place

hostels: places that provide inexpensive lodging

itinerary: a travel route with timings or a specific plan for a trip

sharing economy: a system in which a person is able to borrow or rent items owned by someone else

souvenirs: items that remind people of particular places they have visited

supersonic: able to travel faster than the speed of sound

transcontinental: going or reaching across an entire continent

Index

LIGHTBOX

SUPPLEMENTARY RESOURCES

Click on the plus icon found in the bottom left corner of each spread to open additional teacher resources.

- Download and print the book's quizzes and activities
- Access curriculum correlations
- Explore additional web applications that enhance the Lightbox experience

LIGHTBOX DIGITAL TITLES
Packed full of integrated media

VIDEOS

INTERACTIVE MAPS

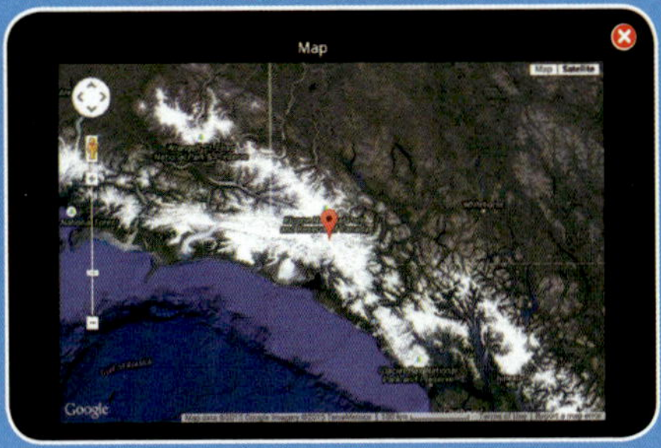

WEBLINKS

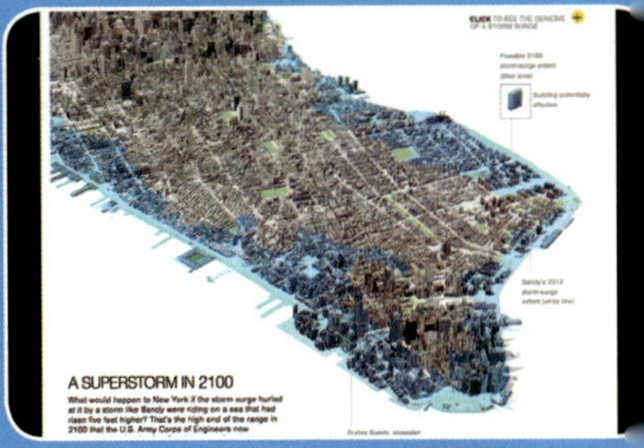

SLIDESHOWS

QUIZZES

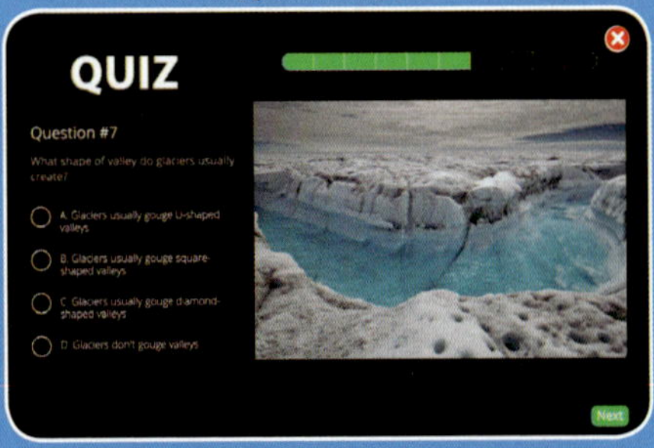

OPTIMIZED FOR

- ✔ TABLETS
- ✔ WHITEBOARDS
- ✔ COMPUTERS
- ✔ AND MUCH MORE!

Published by Smartbook Media Inc.
350 5th Avenue, 59th Floor New York, NY 10118
Website: www.openlightbox.com

Project Coordinator: Heather Kissock
Art Director: Terry Paulhus

Library of Congress Cataloging-in-Publication Data
Names: Truesdale, Lisa, author | Kissock, Heather, author.
Title: Travel and tourism / Lisa Truesdale and Heather Kissock.
Description: New York, NY : Smartbook Media Inc., [2019] | Series: American industries | Includes index.
Identifiers: LCCN 2017060464 (print) | LCCN 2017055656 (ebook) | ISBN 9781510535541 (hardcover : alk. paper) | ISBN 9781510535558 (Multi User ebook)
Subjects: LCSH: Tourism--Juvenile literature.
Classification: LCC G155.A1 T6955 2019 (ebook) | LCC G155.A1 (print) | DDC 910--dc23
LC record available at https://lccn.loc.gov/2017060464

Printed in Brainerd, Minnesota, United States
1 2 3 4 5 6 7 8 9 0 22 21 20 19 18

042018
120517

Every reasonable effort has been made to trace ownership and to obtain permission to reprint copyright material. The publisher would be pleased to have any errors or omissions brought to its attention so that they may be corrected in subsequent printings.
The publisher acknowledges Getty Images, Alamy, Newscom, Shutterstock, and iStock as its primary image suppliers for this title.